VAMPIRE KILLER

'Why do you want this job?' Professor Fletcher asks.

'I need money,' Colin answers.

'Do you believe in vampires?' Fletcher asks.

'Vampires? Are you talking about Dracula?' asks Colin.

'Dracula is a book, but this is true,' says Fletcher. 'There is a vampire here in your town. I must find it and kill it tonight or . . .'

'What is this job?' Colin thinks. He needs a job and he needs money, but this is crazy. Then Colin sees the money in Fletcher's hand – it's a lot of money . . . maybe he *can* do this job. Then he meets Claudia – she is also looking for a job with Professor Fletcher. 'She has a nice smile. She has beautiful eyes too,' Colin thinks.

Is Fletcher crazy? Are there vampires in town? And who is the beautiful Claudia?

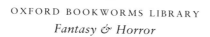

OXFORD BOOKWORMS LIBRARY
Fantasy & Horror

Vampire Killer

Starter (250 headwords)

PAUL SHIPTON

Vampire Killer

Illustrated by
Andy Parker

OXFORD UNIVERSITY PRESS

OXFORD

UNIVERSITY PRESS

Great Clarendon Street, Oxford OX2 6DP

Oxford University Press is a department of the University of Oxford.
It furthers the University's objective of excellence in research, scholarship,
and education by publishing worldwide in

Oxford New York

Auckland Cape Town Dar es Salaam Hong Kong Karachi
Kuala Lumpur Madrid Melbourne Mexico City Nairobi
New Delhi Shanghai Taipei Toronto

With offices in

Argentina Austria Brazil Chile Czech Republic France Greece
Guatemala Hungary Italy Japan Poland Portugal Singapore
South Korea Switzerland Thailand Turkey Ukraine Vietnam

OXFORD and OXFORD ENGLISH are registered trade marks of
Oxford University Press in the UK and in certain other countries

ISBN: 978 0 19 423419 1

Printed in Hong Kong

Word count (main text): 1160

For more information on the Oxford Bookworms Library, visit
www.oup.com/bookworms

CONTENTS

VAMPIRE KILLER

I'm strong, fast and brave . . . I can do this job.

Hello. I'm calling about the job.

Come to 58 Bottle Road.

I can come tomorrow.

Tomorrow's no good. You must come now.

But . . .

Twenty minutes later . . .

DING DONG!

Yes? What do you want?

Professor Fletcher? I'm Colin Miller.

Come in.

Then Fletcher asks the important question.

Do you believe in vampires?

Vampires! Oh dear – this is no good!

It's late! Sorry! I must go now. I –

Wait! You need a job and you need money!

But what is the job?

I am a vampire killer. I find vampires and I kill them . . . And now I need help.

Vampires? Are you talking about Dracula?

It's dark and cold in the street now.

Excuse me.

58

My name's Claudia. I'm here for the job.

Be careful. He's crazy. He's a vampire killer.

Ha! Ha! Vampires? Wonderful! Are you working for him?

Yes . . . but this isn't a joke!

58

OK, but I'm interested. Perhaps he wants another helper?

Colin is tired, but he does not want to go home.

KING'S ARMS

Perhaps one little drink...

Two pounds, please.

I've got no more money now.

Two of Colin's friends are in the pub.

Hi, Colin. Have you got a job now?

Oh ... yes.

What do you do?

I'm a ... a vampire killer.

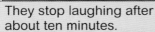

They stop laughing after about ten minutes.

Come here and give me a kiss!

Go away!

Hey! Where are you going?

The supermarket.

But the supermarket's . . .

. . . closed

Oh, no! My watch is slow. I'm late!

Professor Fletcher is not at the supermarket. But someone is waiting there.

The professor does not answer Claudia's question.

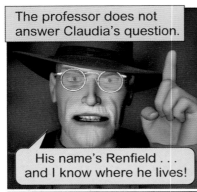

His name's Renfield . . . and I know where he lives!

They run through the dark streets.

This is the street. We can wait here.

So they wait . . .

. . . and wait.

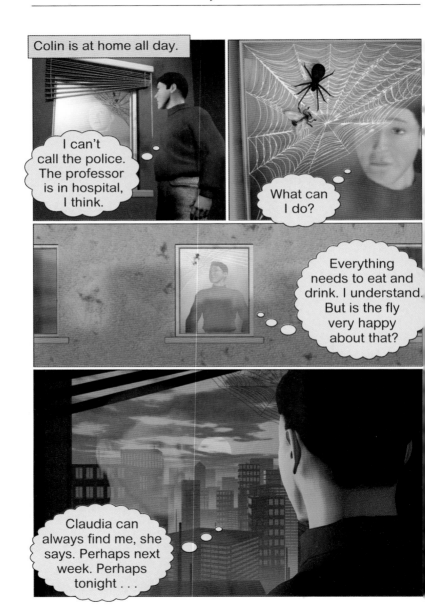

GLOSSARY

believe think that something or someone exists

blood a red liquid in the body

brave *(adj)* not showing or feeling fear

crazy *(adj)* mad or insane

dangerous something that can hurt you is dangerous

doctor a medical person who treats sick people

film a moving picture you see at the cinema

fly a small flying insect

food what people and animals eat

ghost a dead person who appears again

horror the kind of books and films about ghosts and vampires

job work people do to earn money

joke something you say or do to make people laugh

kiss touch with the lips

ouch what you say when you are in pain

professor a teacher at a university

strong *(adj)* having a powerful body

vampire a supernatural creature which drinks the blood of living people

Vampire Killer

ACTIVITIES

ACTIVITIES

Before Reading

1 **Look at the front cover of the book and guess the answers to these questions.**

   1 The story happens . . .

     a ☐ today.

     b ☐ 200 years ago.

     c ☐ not in a or b.

   2 The story happens . . .

     a ☐ in a city.

     b ☐ in the country.

     c ☐ not in a or b.

2 **Read the back cover of the book and choose the correct ending for these sentences.**

   1 Professor Fletcher is . . .

     a ☐ a vampire.

     b ☐ a vampire killer.

     c ☐ a doctor.

   2 At the end of the story I think Colin . . .

     a ☐ finds a vampire.

     b ☐ fights Professor Fletcher.

     c ☐ runs away from the professor.

ACTIVITIES

While Reading

1 Read pages 1–6 then answer these questions.

1 Where does Colin find out about the job?
2 When does the Professor want to see Colin?
3 Is Colin a fast runner?
4 Does Colin believe in vampires?
5 Why does Colin take the job?

2 Read pages 7–12. Are these sentences true (T) or false (F)?

1 ☐ Claudia is not interested in the job.
2 ☐ Colin's friends laugh at his new job.
3 ☐ Colin arrives at the supermarket at midnight.
4 ☐ Colin does not believe in vampires.
5 ☐ Professor Fletcher is waiting at the supermarket.
6 ☐ Claudia is working for the professor too.
7 ☐ Professor Fletcher shows a photograph of the vampire.
8 ☐ Colin likes Claudia.

3 Read pages 13–18. Match the words with the pictures.

a Renfield begins to laugh.

b Just then, they hear a noise.

c The professor drives fast.

d Renfield begins to run.

4 Read pages 19–24 and answer these questions.

1 Where is Colin when he sees the vampire?

2 Who is the vampire?

3 Why can't Professor Fletcher help?

4 Why does Claudia run into the next room?

5 What does Colin do with the Professor?

6 What does Colin want to do at the end of the story?

ACTIVITIES

After Reading

1 **Match the sentence following sentence halves to make five complete sentences.**

   1 Colin takes the job . . .
   2 His friends laugh . . .
   3 Colin is late . . .
   4 Claudia runs away . . .
   5 Colin wants to leave this town . . .

   a because Colin is a vampire killer.
   b because his watch is slow.
   c because he is afraid of Claudia.
   d because he needs money.
   e because she is afraid of the sun.

2 **Complete this summary of the story. Use these words:**

   believe   blood   brave   job   joke   lives   midnight
   money   runs   sun   vampire

   Colin calls Professor Fletcher about a .... Fletcher
   says he is a vampire killer and he needs a helper. The
   helper must be strong, fast and .... Colin does not
   .... in vampires, but he takes the job because he needs
   .... His friends laugh about the job. One of them
   buys some vampire teeth from the .... shop.
   At .... Colin meets the professor outside the

supermarket. Claudia is there too. They find a man called
Renfield. Renfield tells them where the vampire ....
At the flat, Colin learns something – Claudia is the
.... ! She wants to drink Colin's .... But suddenly
the .... comes up. Colin .... away.

3 **Write a different ending by filling in the speech bubbles.**

4 **What happens when Claudia and Colin meet again? Write
and draw a new ending for the story.**

. . . .
. . . .
. . . .
. . . .
. . . .

ABOUT THE AUTHOR

Paul Shipton taught English in Turkey and the UK for several years, and then he became an editor of school books in the UK and the US. He lived in the US for ten years in Chicago and then Wisconsin. He has recently returned to England and now lives in Cambridge with his wife and two daughters. He is now a full-time writer and has written almost one hundred books, most of them fiction for children. One of his books, *Bug Muldoon and the Garden of Fear*, received the Austrian Children's Book Award in 2002. Paul wrote Vampire Killer because he wanted to write a modern version of a good, old-fashioned scary story.

OXFORD BOOKWORMS LIBRARY

Classics • Crime & Mystery • Factfiles • Fantasy & Horror
Human Interest • Playscripts • Thriller & Adventure
True Stories • World Stories

The OXFORD BOOKWORMS LIBRARY provides enjoyable reading in English, with a wide range of classic and modern fiction, non-fiction, and plays. It includes original and adapted texts in seven carefully graded language stages, which take learners from beginner to advanced level. An overview is given on the next pages.

All Stage 1 titles are available as audio recordings, as well as over eighty other titles from Starter to Stage 6. All Starters and many titles at Stages 1 to 4 are specially recommended for younger learners. Every Bookworm is illustrated, and Starters and Factfiles have full-colour illustrations.

The OXFORD BOOKWORMS LIBRARY also offers extensive support. Each book contains an introduction to the story, notes about the author, a glossary, and activities. Additional resources include tests and worksheets, and answers for these and for the activities in the books. There is advice on running a class library, using audio recordings, and the many ways of using Oxford Bookworms in reading programmes. Resource materials are available on the website <www.oup.com/bookworms>.

The *Oxford Bookworms Collection* is a series for advanced learners. It consists of volumes of short stories by well-known authors, both classic and modern. Texts are not abridged or adapted in any way, but carefully selected to be accessible to the advanced student.

You can find details and a full list of titles in the *Oxford Bookworms Library Catalogue* and *Oxford English Language Teaching Catalogues*, and on the website <www.oup.com/bookworms>.

THE OXFORD BOOKWORMS LIBRARY
GRADING AND SAMPLE EXTRACTS

STARTER • 250 HEADWORDS

present simple – present continuous – imperative –
can/cannot, must – *going to* (future) – simple gerunds …

Her phone is ringing – but where is it?

Sally gets out of bed and looks in her bag. No phone. She looks under the bed. No phone. Then she looks behind the door. There is her phone. Sally picks up her phone and answers it. ***Sally's Phone***

STAGE 1 • 400 HEADWORDS

… past simple – coordination with *and, but, or* –
subordination with *before, after, when, because, so* …

I knew him in Persia. He was a famous builder and I worked with him there. For a time I was his friend, but not for long. When he came to Paris, I came after him – I wanted to watch him. He was a very clever, very dangerous man. ***The Phantom of the Opera***

STAGE 2 • 700 HEADWORDS

… present perfect – *will* (future) – *(don't) have to, must not, could* – comparison of adjectives – simple *if* clauses – past continuous – tag questions – *ask/tell* + infinitive …

While I was writing these words in my diary, I decided what to do. I must try to escape. I shall try to get down the wall outside. The window is high above the ground, but I have to try. I shall take some of the gold with me – if I escape, perhaps it will be helpful later. ***Dracula***

STAGE 3 • 1000 HEADWORDS

... should, may – present perfect continuous – *used to* – past perfect –
causative – relative clauses – indirect statements ...

Of course, it was most important that no one should see
Colin, Mary, or Dickon entering the secret garden. So Colin
gave orders to the gardeners that they must all keep away
from that part of the garden in future. ***The Secret Garden***

STAGE 4 • 1400 HEADWORDS

... past perfect continuous – passive (simple forms) –
would conditional clauses – indirect questions –
relatives with *where/when* – gerunds after prepositions/phrases ...

I was glad. Now Hyde could not show his face to the world
again. If he did, every honest man in London would be
proud to report him to the police. ***Dr Jekyll and Mr Hyde***

STAGE 5 • 1800 HEADWORDS

... future continuous – future perfect –
passive (modals, continuous forms) –
would have conditional clauses – modals + perfect infinitive ...

If he had spoken Estella's name, I would have hit him. I was so
angry with him, and so depressed about my future, that I could
not eat the breakfast. Instead I went straight to the old house.
Great Expectations

STAGE 6 • 2500 HEADWORDS

... passive (infinitives, gerunds) – advanced modal meanings –
clauses of concession, condition

When I stepped up to the piano, I was confident. It was as if I
knew that the prodigy side of me really did exist. And when I
started to play, I was so caught up in how lovely I looked that
I didn't worry how I would sound. ***The Joy Luck Club***

BOOKWORMS · FANTASY & HORROR · STARTER

New York Café

MICHAEL DEAN

It is the year 2030, and an e-mail message arrives at New York Café: 'I want to help people and make them happy!' But not everybody is happy about the e-mail, and soon the police and the President are very interested in the New York Café.

BOOKWORMS · FANTASY & HORROR · STARTER

Starman

PHILLIP BURROWS AND MARK FOSTER

The empty centre of Australia. The sun is hot and there are not many people. And when Bill meets a man, alone, standing on an empty road a long way from anywhere, he is surprised and worried.

And Bill is right to be worried. Because there is something strange about the man he meets. Very strange . . .

BOOKWORMS · HUMAN INTEREST · STARTER

King Arthur

JANET HARDY-GOULD

It is the year 650 in England. There is war everywhere because the old king is dead and he has no son. Only when the new king comes can the fighting stop and the strange, magical story of King Arthur begin. But first, Merlin the ancient magician has to find a way of finding the next king . . .

BOOKWORMS · THRILLER & ADVENTURE · STARTER

The White Stones

LESTER VAUGHAN

'The people on this island don't like archaeologists,' the woman on the ferry says. You only want to study the 4,500 year-old Irish megalithic stones but very soon strange things begin to happen to you. Can you solve the mystery in time?

BOOKWORMS · FANTASY & HORROR · STAGE 1

The Monkey's Paw

W. W. JACOBS

Retold by Diane Mowat

Outside, the night is cold and wet. Inside, the White family sits and waits. Where is their visitor?

There is a knock at the door. A man is standing outside in the dark. Their visitor has arrived.

The visitor waits. He has been in India for many years. What has he got? He has brought the hand of a small, dead animal – a monkey's paw.

Outside, in the dark, the visitor smiles and waits for the door to open.

BOOKWORMS · FANTASY & HORROR · STAGE 1

The Phantom of the Opera

JENNIFER BASSETT

It is 1880, in the Opera House in Paris. Everybody is talking about the Phantom of the Opera, the ghost that lives somewhere under the Opera House. The Phantom is a man in black clothes. He is a body without a head, he is a head without a body. He has a yellow face, he has no nose, he has black holes for eyes. Everybody is afraid of the Phantom – the singers, the dancers, the directors, the Stage workers . . .

But who has actually seen him?

"Andy can run really, really fast." He pointed to another.

"You certainly know a lot about everyone," said Mrs. Little.

"I've been here awhile," said Stuart softly.

Something in his voice touched Mr. and Mrs. Little.

It didn't take long for them to make up their minds.

They told Mrs. Keeper, the woman
in charge of the orphanage, that they
wanted to adopt Stuart.

"There is a good chance this will not
work out!" she told them sternly.

After all, Stuart was a mouse, and
the Littles were people.

But the Littles had come to love
Stuart in a few short minutes, and they
were certain he would fit right in with
their family.

So, they took Stuart home.